FIRST-PERSON STORIES OF THE
COVID-19 PANDEMIC

BY NICOLE HORNING

ROSEN PUBLISHING PRIMARY SOURCE LIBRARY

ROSEN PUBLISHING

Published in 2027 by The Rosen Publishing Group, Inc.
2544 Clinton Street, Buffalo, NY 14224

Designer: Deanna Lepovich
Editor: Nicole Horning

Cataloging-in-Publication Data

Names: Horning, Nicole.
Title: First-person stories of the COVID-19 pandemic / Nicole Horning.
Description: Buffalo, NY : Rosen Publishing, 2027. | Series: The Rosen Publishing primary source library | Includes glossary and index.
Identifiers: ISBN 9781725343108 (pbk.) | ISBN 9781725343115 (library bound) | ISBN 9781725343122 (ebook)
Subjects: LCSH: COVID-19 Pandemic, 2020-2023–Juvenile literature. | COVID-19 (Disease)–Social aspects–United States–Juvenile literature. | COVID-19 (Disease)–Juvenile literature.
Classification: LCC RA644.C67H67 2027 | DDC 614.592414–dc23

Some of the images in this book illustrate individuals who are models. The depictions do not imply actual situations or events.

Manufactured in the United States of America

CPSIA Compliance Information: Batch #CSRYA27. For further information, contact Rosen Publishing at 1-800-237-9932.

CONTENTS

FOREWORD

History is so much more than just a boring collection of names and dates. It is a collection of stories—sometimes tragic stories, sometimes heroic stories, sometimes romantic stories, sometimes scary stories. And they're all stories of real people who lived real lives.

Those stories can get lost in the shuffle of memorizing battles, studying maps, and listing important court cases or rulers. That's why primary sources are so valuable. They remind us that historical events happened to and because of real people. Reading diaries, looking at photographs, and seeing newspaper articles are just some ways to make history feel personal through primary sources.

Another way is through watching or listening to interviews with people who lived through major historical events. That's what you're invited to do in this book—and all the books that are part of the *Rosen Publishing Primary Source Library*. Each chapter includes quotes from an interview with a real person who experienced a major historical event in a deeply personal way. You can also scan the QR code included at the beginning of each chapter to watch a video interview with the person featured in that chapter.

Created in partnership with Generations Broadcasting, the *Rosen Publishing Primary Source Library* was created to remind readers that there is power in sharing our stories. First-person stories make history come alive. And when history comes alive, we're better able to learn from it—and avoid the mistakes of the past.

The events you're living through today will be part of the next generation's history lessons. As you read and watch the stories collected here, think about what you want your story to be.

Note: More interviews about the topics featured in this series, as well as many other historical events, can be accessed via a subscription to Rosen Publishing's GBC Stories Database: rosendigital.com/GBCStories/.

HOW TO WATCH THE INTERVIEWS FEATURED IN THIS BOOK

- Use your phone's camera, and hold it over the QR code.
- Click the link that appears.
- Watch the video that pops up. If you would like to read a transcript of the interview while you watch, you can click on that option using the menu on the video screen.

INTRODUCTION

In late 2019, a new virus began spreading around the world. People were becoming very sick, and doctors didn't know how to help them. It wasn't long after the virus emerged in 2019 that life as people knew it shut down, changing lives for years to come.

The sickness caused by this virus, known as COVID-19 because it started in 2019, caused a global pandemic that resulted in schools closing down, hospitals being filled to capacity, the end of travel, and families being separated from one another to help prevent the spread of the disease. Sporting events were also canceled, workplaces moved online, and public spaces that brought people together like coffeeshops or stores were empty to also prevent the spread of COVID-19. Because of this, many small businesses were heavily impacted and shut down for good either during the worst years of the pandemic or shortly after. The world seemed to change overnight.

As the pandemic went on, doctors and scientists learned more about COVID-19. For example, it was discovered that COVID-19 mainly spreads through close contact with people, often before people even know they are sick. Because the virus has a long **incubation period** of between two and fourteen days, with many people developing symptoms around day five, it made the virus incredibly difficult to control. Additionally, in the beginning of the pandemic, there weren't treatments or vaccines developed, so there was a lot of fear in society of becoming sick with the disease, especially if someone's immune system was **compromised**.

Because the virus was so new and spread so rapidly, doctors and scientists didn't fully understand how it spread or how to treat it. Governments had to make difficult decisions quickly, often with limited information. As a result, rules and advice frequently changed as people learned more about the virus.

Doctors and nurses had to rely on very limited information while caring for patients, often only being able to treat the symptoms of the disease. Additionally, they had to care for growing numbers of patients during very long hospital shifts. Hospitals also faced shortages of protective equipment such as masks or gloves, meaning healthcare workers had to work long hours under dangerous conditions.

Masking was key to trying to end the pandemic, which was caused by a virus known as SARS-CoV-2.

Many health-care workers themselves became sick while trying to help these patients.

The COVID-19 pandemic largely took place from 2020 through 2021, with the World Health Organization (WHO) declaring an end to the public health emergency in May 2023. However, many of its effects are still felt today, especially for those who lost loved ones due to COVID-19.

Because COVID-19 was a new disease, scientists and doctors were learning about it in real time. They studied how it spread, who was most at risk, and which treatments worked best, and they eventually developed a vaccine to help prevent or lessen the effects of COVID-19.

The pandemic revealed how connected the world truly is. A virus that started in one place was able to quickly make its way around the world through global travel. At the same time, the virus showed how people responded to crises in different ways and how **resilient** people were in the face of a frightening disease, loneliness, and stress.

CHAPTER ONE

A NEW VIRUS

In the early days of the COVID-19 pandemic, people around the world were learning about the mysterious virus SARS-CoV-2 through news reports, rumors, and scattered information. Doctors and nurses were among the first people to face the reality of COVID-19 before clear rules, treatments, or protections were in place. They, like the rest of the world, were learning about the virus at the same time as everyone else and discovering what worked to help patients through trial and error. In an interview, an anonymous nurse described what it was like to be a health-care worker in the early days of the pandemic.

WHAT COVID-19 IS

COVID-19 is caused by a virus, which is a tiny infectious agent that survives and multiplies inside living cells. Some viruses cause mild illnesses, such as the common cold, while others, like SARS-CoV-2, are much more dangerous. COVID-19 is caused by a coronavirus, which is a type of virus that's named for it crown-like spikes.

There are two main theories for how the virus originated. The first theory is it spread through animals, jumping from bats to people, similar to how severe acute respiratory syndrome (SARS) and Middle

Scan this QR code to watch a nurse talk about the early days of the COVID-19 pandemic.

East respiratory syndrome (MERS) developed. The other theory is there was a laboratory leak from a type of coronavirus being studied on animals. However, COVID-19 was not **genetically engineered** or created to be a **biological weapon**.

FAST FACT

A PANDEMIC IS AN OUTBREAK OF A DISEASE THAT SPREADS ACROSS MANY COUNTRIES AND AFFECTS A LARGE NUMBER OF PEOPLE. COVID-19 WAS DECLARED A PANDEMIC IN MARCH 2020.

COVID-19 first appeared in December 2019 with a cluster of cases in Wuhan, China. At the beginning of the pandemic, it was first believed that COVID-19 made the jump to humans at a wet market in Wuhan. Wet markets are open-air markets that sell fresh meat and produce. The WHO in China discovered several illnesses like pneumonia that seemed to be connected to this market and included symptoms like fever and shortness of breath. However, as COVID-19 spread across the world, people

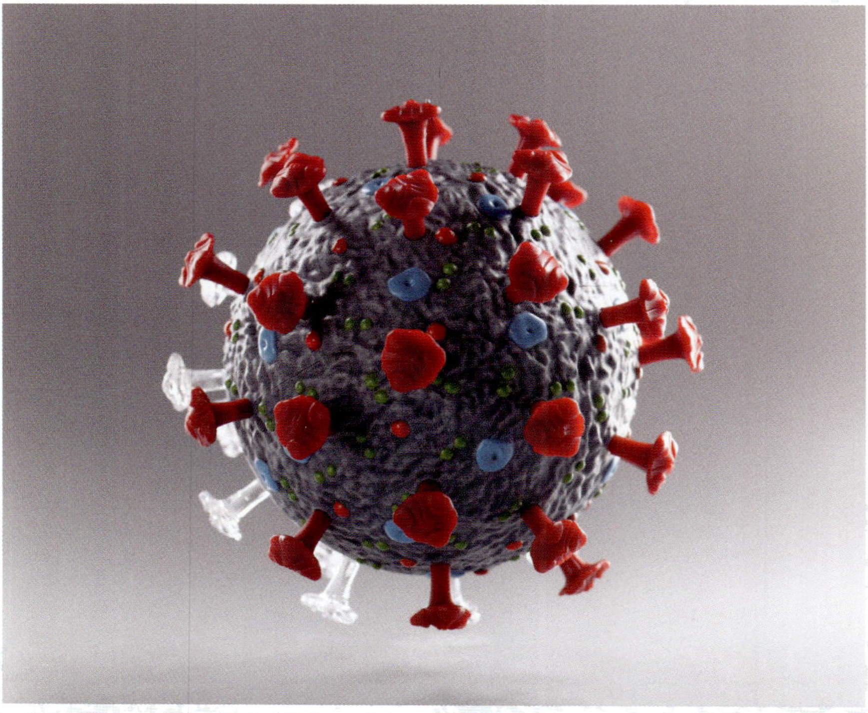

A COVID-19 virus model is shown here.

FAST FACT

ONE OF THE MOST FAMOUS PANDEMICS IN HISTORY WAS THE 1918 INFLUENZA PANDEMIC, WHICH THE COVID-19 PANDEMIC WAS FREQUENTLY COMPARED TO. IT INFECTED ABOUT ONE-THIRD OF THE POPULATION AND CAUSED MILLIONS OF DEATHS.

were becoming infected who had no contact with animals, which showed it was spreading between humans.

What made COVID-19 so dangerous is that it was new. Because this virus wasn't encountered before, people had no **immunity** to it. There were no vaccines or proven treatments when it first appeared. Because of this, the virus spread quickly and caused serious illness

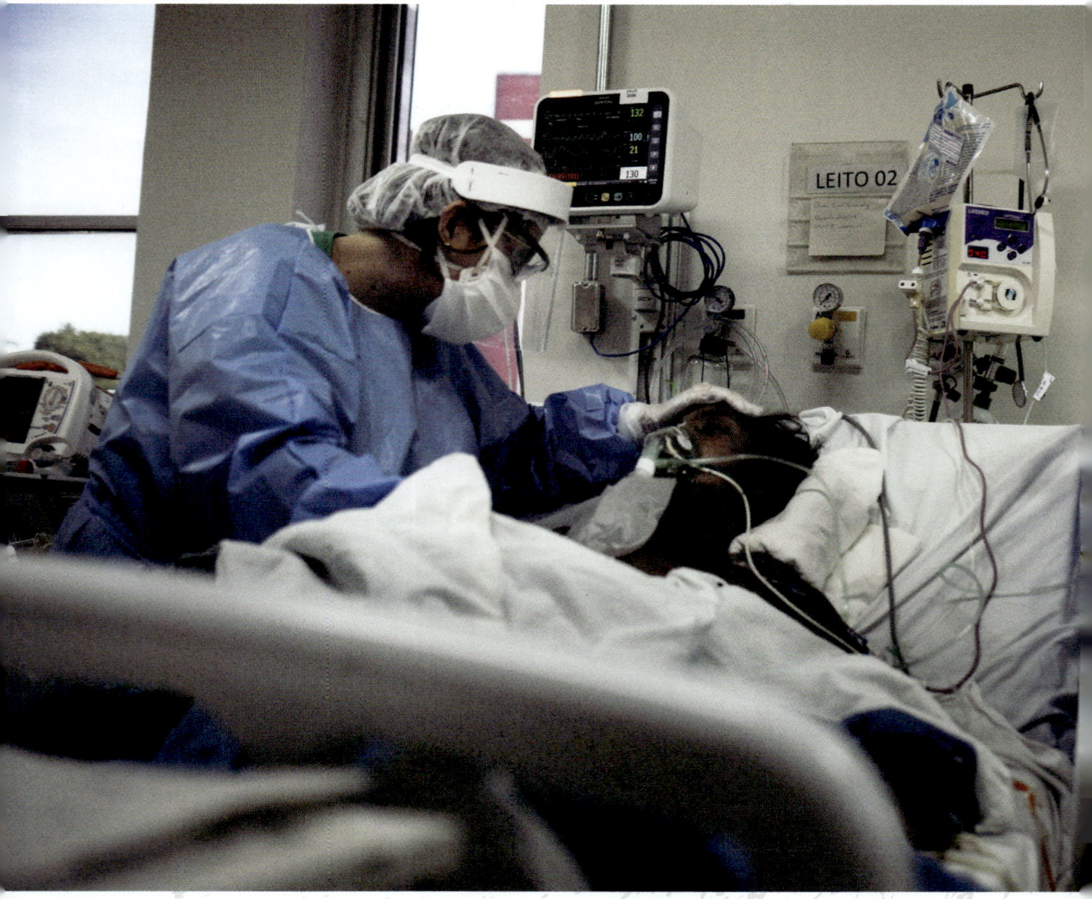

A doctor is shown here caring for a patient with COVID-19.

in many people, especially the elderly and people with existing health conditions such as asthma.

FIRST CASES

In December 2019, doctors in Wuhan started noticing unusual cases of pneumonia. Patients were showing serious breathing problems, but the cause was unclear. By January 2020, scientists confirmed that a new coronavirus was the reason for this illness and warned that it could spread easily from person to person.

In an interview, one nurse recalled what it was like in the early days of the pandemic, treating their first patient:

> *And of course, when the COVID hits in March, when we started having this patient at the VA [Veterans Affrais hospital], one of the things about the VA is we only entertain the VA patients. So we don't have that many initially because he's only the veteran I have to deal with. But our ground zero patient that we admitted in [the] ICU, that's the big ... the scariest thing that everybody felt in the unit. It was like, ER is calling. We have this patient [with] possible COVID-19, and we have [them] in our isolation room. And then all of us were like, I, I hope it's not my patient ... And for that kind of patient that we have for the first time in the hospital, three of our medical people got infected, and that scares all of us and me.*

For hospitals, "ground zero" meant their first confirmed case. Before vaccines were developed and more was learned about the virus, early patients with COVID-19 often required intensive care, including ventilators to help them breathe. And because so little was known about the virus and how to prevent transmission, doctors and nurses feared becoming infected themselves, especially when they were seeing firsthand how the disease was impacting people.

FAST FACT

SARS-COV-2 IS THE NAME OF THE VIRUS THAT CAUSES COVID-19, WHICH IS THE DISEASE. IF A PERSON CATCHES THE SARS-COV-2 VIRUS, THEY BECOME SICK WITH THE DISEASE KNOWN AS COVID-19.

People who weren't in the same family stayed separated from each other on public transportation during the pandemic. Stickers were placed where people weren't supposed to sit.

WHY THE WORLD DIDN'T REACT RIGHT AWAY

There are several reasons why the virus spread so quickly before strong action was taken. One reason is global travel. People move between countries every day, and with how long it took for symptoms to appear, people were spreading the virus without even knowing they had it yet.

Another challenge was conflicting information. Governments and health organizations were trying to understand the virus at the same time it was spreading, and some governments were stricter than others when it came to containing the virus. For example, in the United States, there was a delayed response to starting COVID-19 testing, poor communication, and a delay in implementing lockdowns. Additionally, a large number of people didn't believe COVID-19 was even real or thought that its severity was exaggerated. This made it even harder to implement measures that would keep people safe and help prevent the spread of the disease.

People loaded up their carts at the grocery store, worried that necessities would run out and they would be without them. However, this buying behavior is what led to the shortages.

COMPARING COVID-19 TO PAST DISEASES

Some health-care workers compared COVID-19 to earlier diseases they had encountered, such as tuberculosis (TB), which also spreads through the air. In her interview, the nurse said:

> *Growing up in the Philippines, I had to deal with TB, which is ... almost the same as the COVID thing, but, you know COVID is worse ... But every day coming to work, it is always scary.*

SHORTAGES IN NECESSARY MATERIALS

During the pandemic, there was a massive shortage of personal protective equipment (PPE) such as masks, gowns, and gloves due to a huge increase in demand, disrupted supply chains, and an **insufficient** number of these items in storage. Hospital workers and first responders had to deal with this shortage, leading the Centers for Disease Control and Prevention (CDC) to advise on how they could conserve these items. As a result, health-care workers had to reuse items such as N95 masks, which posed a large threat to their safety and reduced how effective they could be in their response to the pandemic.

"Panic buying" from consumers led to shortages of other kinds of goods. They purchased a large amount of the same item at one time, thinking there would be a shortage later. However, this panic buying behavior created shortages because manufacturers couldn't keep up with the large increase in demand. Items that were panic bought during the pandemic included toilet paper, painkillers, hand sanitizer, rubbing alcohol, antibacterial wipes, bottled water, milk, and masks. As a result of people overbuying, stores started to limit the sale of these items, only allowing consumers to purchase a certain amount at one time.

Because of panic buying, some stores placed signs in and outside of the the store telling people what items they were sold out of.

Online retailers like Amazon also had problems with these kinds of goods because people were selling them at a much higher price than normal because of the demand, which is known as price gouging.

It was common to see empty shelves like this during the pandemic because people bought multiples of the same item.

COVID-19 was different than other diseases health-care workers had seen before. It spread faster, sometimes from people who didn't feel sick at all. This made it harder to control and even more frightening to face.

Many people carried masks and hand sanitizer in the car with them during the COVID-19 pandemic. This helped keep them and others safe.

HOW YOU SEE HISTORY

1. Why is factual information so important during a public health crisis?
2. How does uncertainty change the way people react to danger?
3. What are your most vivid memories of the early days of the COVID-19 pandemic?

CHAPTER TWO

THE HUMAN IMPACT

When COVID-19 started spreading rapidly in 2020, public health officials took steps to slow the spread of the virus. These actions changed how people lived their daily lives almost immediately. Events were canceled, schools closed, workplaces moved to work-from-home setups, and people were told to stay home to prevent further spread of the virus. These changes were meant to protect public health, but they also had a large impact on mental health and connection for people of all ages and from all walks of life. For example, in an interview, Odessa, who is a founder of the Women's National Football Conference, talked about how the pandemic changed her life and how she felt during this time.

LOCKDOWN ORDERS

In March 2020, many U.S. states issued stay-at-home orders, often called lockdowns. The orders asked people to only leave their homes for essential reasons, such as buying food or receiving medical care. Schools closed and switched to lessons delivered through video platforms such as Zoom, and if it was possible, many businesses also switched to a remote work setup with meetings happening via video.

Scan this QR code to watch Odessa talk about her experience dealing with the COVID-19 pandemic.

It was common to see signs such as this one reminding people what to do to stop the spread of COVID-19.

FAST FACT

SOME WORKERS WERE CONSIDERED ESSENTIAL, SO THEY COULDN'T WORK FROM HOME EVEN WHEN MOST BUSINESSES CLOSED. THEY INCLUDED HEALTH-CARE WORKERS, GROCERY STORE WORKERS, AND PUBLIC TRANSPORTATION WORKERS.

Large gatherings such as weddings were canceled, postponed, or changed to a different format. In some cases, there were rules for how many people could gather in one space. In many instances, people had to wear face masks in public settings.

Lockdowns were designed to limit close

Stores used markers on the floor to promote social distancing.

contact between people because COVID-19 spreads most easily when people are near one another for extended periods of time, especially indoors. By reducing gatherings and encouraging people to only be around those who lived in their house, officials hoped to slow the spread of the virus and prevent hospitals from becoming overwhelmed.

THE LOSS OF ROUTINE

Sporting events, concerts, plays, and movies were canceled because they brought people together. Even small gatherings were considered risky, so a lot of events were canceled altogether or moved online.

For many people, these events were more than just entertainment. They were important milestones, like graduations;

All around the world, people were reminded to stay a safe distance away from each other.

People were encouraged not to travel unless it was necessary during the pandemic.

a source of connection; or a thing that they enjoyed that gave them hope. People did what they could to hold onto hope during the pandemic when things felt frightening and uncertain, but it was not always easy.

In an interview, Odessa described how the sudden shutdown affected her life:

> *Football was canceled for me. So that's a major life event. Also I traveled a lot. So the idea of being home this much and being* ***resigned*** *to my thoughts, and as an athlete and as a coach, not being able to run around on the field ... I think everyone has their thing that gives them hope ... for me, football is that thing. I've been an athlete my entire life. So not being able to be out on a football field running around after being in the sun for over a decade was* ***traumatic****. And I know that seems so superficial because*

It was common to see chairs and tables spread far apart from each other for social distancing.

FAST FACT

"QUARANTINE" AND "ISOLATION" ARE OFTEN USED TOGETHER, BUT THEY AREN'T THE SAME. QUARANTINE MEANS STAYING AWAY FROM OTHERS AFTER POSSIBLE EXPOSURE TO AN ILLNESS. ISOLATION MEANS TOTALLY SEPARATING FROM OTHERS AFTER TESTING POSITIVE.

a lot of people are going through a lot of things, right? Losing their jobs, losing their homes. But we all have our thing. We all have that one thing that you could go to for your hope.

As an athlete and coach, Odessa had spent years on the field surrounded by teammates and players.

When this ended suddenly, she lost a major part of her identity. Like many others, she found herself at home, separated from routines and activities that gave her purpose and joy.

SOCIAL ISOLATION AND MENTAL HEALTH

While lockdowns were meant to keep people safe, especially if their immune system was compromised, they also had

There were a lot of unknowns during the early days of the pandemic, including how COVID-19 spread. One of the things people started using were tools such as this so they didn't have to touch buttons, screens, or door handles in public.

UNEQUAL IMPACTS OF THE COVID-19 PANDEMIC

The COVID-19 pandemic affected people around the world, but the impact wasn't the same for everyone. Social and economic inequalities meant that some communities had greater risks and challenges than others.

Many people from **marginalized** communities were more likely to be admitted to hospitals and die from COVID-19. Access to health care played a large role in this, with many people not having access to a nearby hospital or not having health insurance. Additionally, many people of color distrust the health-care system because of the racism, **discrimination**, and unethical treatment they have been subjected to by the medical community throughout history. For example, people of color have previously been experimented on in research studies without their **consent**, which has made each generation after these studies wary of doctors and scientists. Many people of color also say they have to speak up to receive the care they need. Many also state that their pain isn't taken seriously, and their requests are ignored because of their race.

These concerns also came up when clinical research studies for the COVID-19 vaccine were starting. A diverse group of people was necessary for scientists to study the effects of COVID-19 vaccines and to see if the vaccines were effective at preventing infection. However, this history of experimentation and mistrust made people not want to join these studies.

Additionally, people in marginalized communities often experienced social inequalities such as living in crowded conditions, having limited access to COVID-19 testing, and working in public-facing jobs such as those in grocery stores or transportation services that didn't allow enough physical distancing. These factors contributed to higher infection rates and more severe outcomes for many people in these communities. Limited access to health care, greater exposure through work and housing, and historical mistrust of medical systems combined to increase risk during the pandemic for people in marginalized groups.

People would sometimes wear gloves in public spaces like grocery stores to help protect themselves from COVID-19, but then they would toss them on the ground afterward, which hurt the environment and was a potential health and safety hazard.

an impact on mental health. People were asked not to hug each other or shake hands. "Social distancing" became a frequent term used during the pandemic to reinforce this idea. Instead of a hug or shaking hands, people fist bumped or touched their elbows. They also were told to maintain a distance of at least 6 feet (1.8 m) from another person. When that was not possible, barriers, dividers, or screens were sometimes used to separate people and avoid the transfer of germs.

Stores and offices had markers showing the direction that people should walk in so they didn't bump into each other.

FAST FACT

LOCKDOWNS WEREN'T PERMANENT. HOW LONG THEY LASTED AND OTHER RESTRICTIONS DEPENDED ON THE NUMBER OF COVID-19 CASES, HOSPITAL CAPACITY, AND COVID-19 TESTING AVAILABILITY.

Without daily in-person interactions, many people experienced rising levels of **anxiety** and **depression**. Routines that helped structure the day such as traveling to a job or school were suddenly gone. For **extroverted** people, the lack of in-person contact was especially difficult. In her interview, Odessa talked about the mental effects of the pandemic:

People ... can't go to church and be close to one another. I haven't seen my church family since January ... And so I think that for me as an extrovert and as a coach and as somebody who inspires and loves to get that—you know I love hugging people and fist bumping and chest bumping and touching folks, so I'm a hands-on person—so for me, it's been quite traumatic ... but it has also made me refocus on what matters to me.

Even during all of this, people found new ways to connect such as video calls, virtual classrooms, and online meetings.

Public spaces installed plastic barriers and also used tables to protect workers and keep a safe distance.

Some parks, like this one in Germany, had circles marked where people should sit for social distancing.

Technology helped people stay in touch, but it couldn't fully replace being together in person.

HOW YOU SEE HISTORY

1. Talk to a parent or guardian about their experiences during the pandemic. Did they struggle with feeling isolated? Did you struggle with those feelings during that time?
2. How might lockdowns have affected people differently depending on their personalities?
3. How did the loss of routines contribute to mental health challenges during the pandemic?

CHAPTER THREE

HEALTH-CARE AND SCIENCE CHALLENGES

Because COVID-19 was considered "novel," or new, there was a lot that scientists, doctors, and public health officials didn't know and were learning in real time as the pandemic progressed and the virus **mutated** into different variants. Additionally, the virus affected people differently, with some people not developing symptoms or an infection even after being exposed to someone who had symptoms and tested positive. Physicians like Dr. Koyi Ugboma were frightened because there was a lot that was unknown. In an interview from 2020, Dr. Ugboma discussed the uncertainty of the pandemic and the initial lack of knowledge about the virus that caused it.

STUDYING THE VIRUS'S SPREAD

Epidemiology is essential to public health. It's the study of health-related conditions such as COVID-19, including identifying risk factors, tracking disease outbreaks, and implementing preventive measures that help stop it from spreading more.

COVID-19 challenged epidemiologists, other scientists, doctors, and traditional research methods from the start. In Dr. Ugboma's interview from 2020, he said:

Scan this QR code to watch Dr. Koyi Ugboma talk about the lack of knowledge about COVID-19 in the summer of 2020.

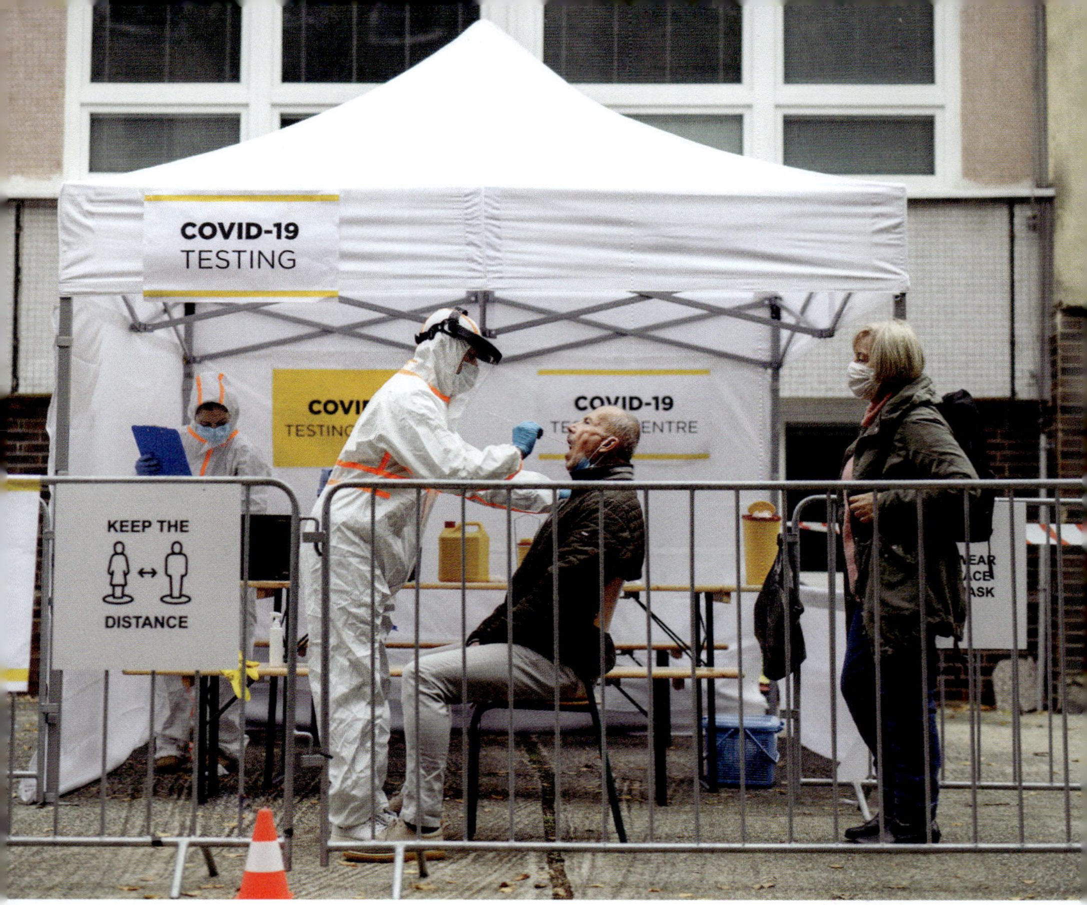

Testing centers such as this one were common throughout the pandemic.

FAST FACT

EARLY COVID-19 TESTS WERE HARD TO FIND BECAUSE CREATING A RELIABLE TEST TAKES A LOT OF TIME. SCIENTISTS HAD TO MAKE SURE IT DETECTED THE RIGHT VIRUS AND DIDN'T CONFUSE IT WITH OTHERS. ADDITIONALLY, EARLY TESTS WERE SLOW TO PRODUCE AND REQUIRED SPECIAL EQUIPMENT, WHICH LIMITED HOW MANY PEOPLE COULD BE TESTED AT ONE TIME.

We're dealing with something very, very dangerous. And I'm very frightened, and most physicians will tell you they're frightened for the first time ... How can something start in Wuhan in China and affect only 20 percent of the geographical location in China ... 80 percent of China is free. In England, it affected the whole country. In the

[United] States, it's affected all the states, but in China, it's only affected 20 percent of the regions of China. So that tells you that something [is] not quite right.

One reason for the fear surrounding COVID-19 was how unevenly the virus spread. Some areas had an overwhelming amount of cases, while others had far fewer. Early data also raised confusing questions: Why did the United States have cases in every state, while other countries only had a small percentage of regions affected? Why did some people have a severe form of the disease, while others didn't get infected at

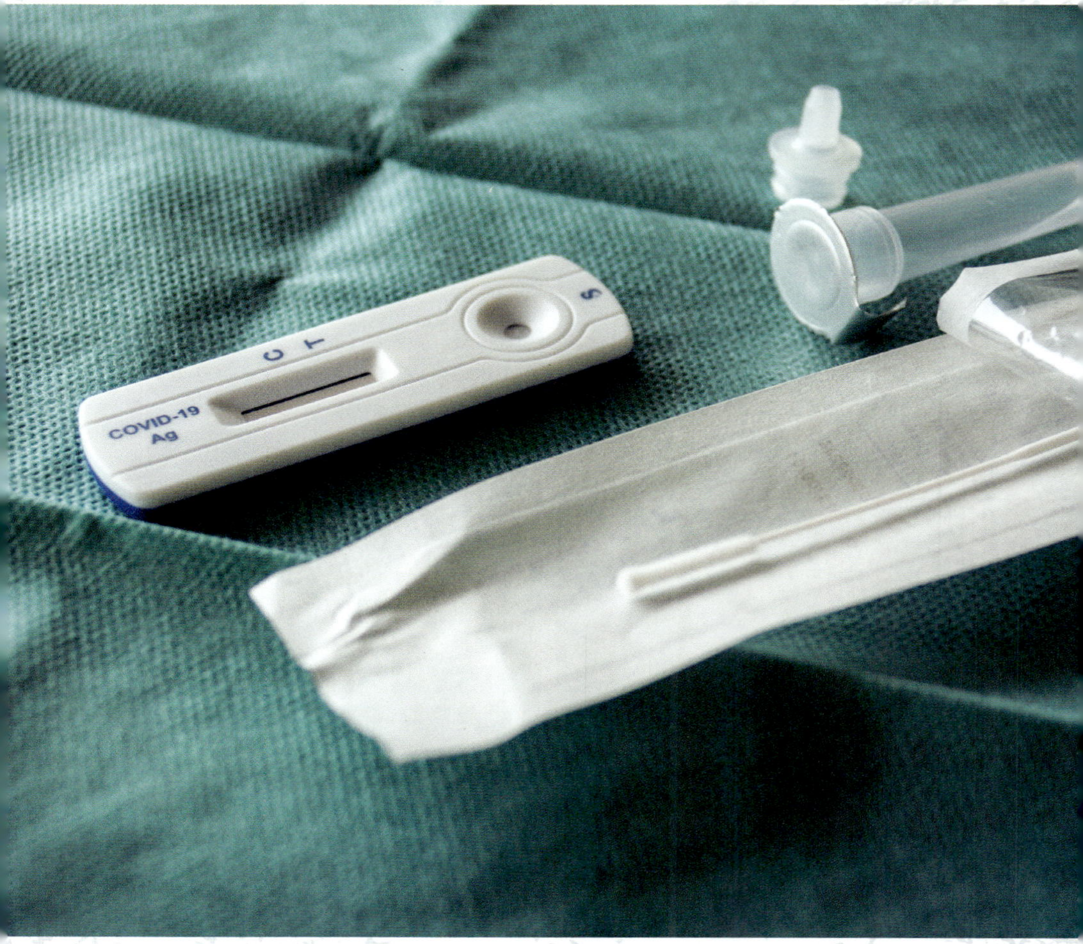

Once COVID-19 tests were perfected and approved, people were able to use rapid at-home tests such as this one to see if they had COVID-19.

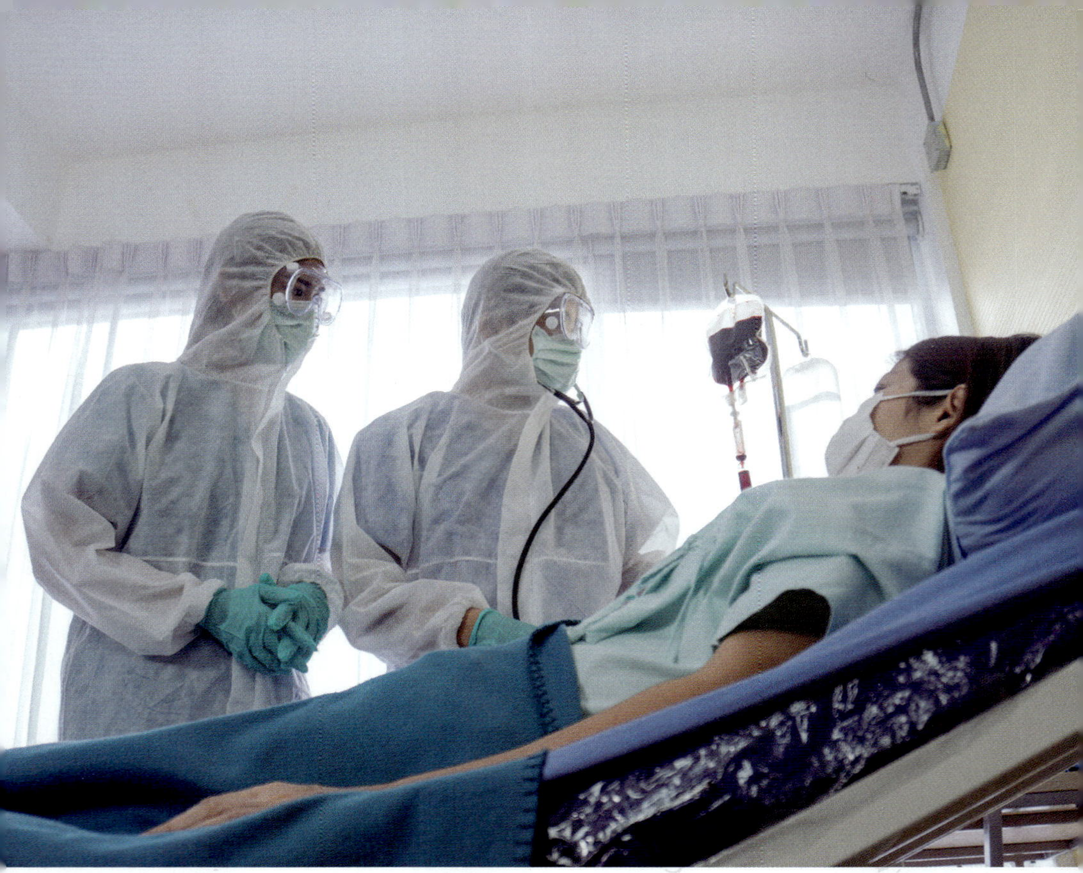

Hospitals took extra protective measures to do what they could to help contain COVID-19 infections and stop the virus from spreading.

FAST FACT

EARLY IN THE PANDEMIC, OFFICIALS USED THE PHRASE "FLATTEN THE CURVE." THIS REFERS TO A GRAPH SHOWING HOW QUICKLY COVID-19 CASES COULD RISE AND OVERWHELM HOSPITALS. SLOWING THE SPREAD HELPED HEALTH-CARE SYSTEMS TREAT EACH PATIENT MORE EFFECTIVELY.

all? These inconsistencies made it hard for officials and scientists to predict what would happen next.

ASYMPTOMATIC CARRIERS

Another issue was asymptomatic spread, in which people who had no symptoms at all still had the virus and were able to infect others. Traditional disease control strategies, like isolating visibly sick patients, didn't

Pharmacies started offering walk-in testing and vaccines to help stop further spread of COVID-19.

work in these cases because people weren't even aware that they were carrying the virus. In his interview, Dr. Ugboma said:

> *What's happening in the [United] States will tell you that even the epidemiology of COVID-19, or coronavirus, we don't ... know about it. Even the world of transmission ... I don't think we know too much about it. We just do what we're told. Wash your hands, use the sanitizer ... We know, for example, that the quantity of virus*

Masks started to be made in different colors and designs to encourage people to wear them.

you take and the duration the virus stays in you are the two most important killer elements in this virus. So what [you have to do] is to reduce the amount of viral load you have, to reduce the amount of contact you have, [and] to reduce the amount of contacted people you think could be asymptomatic carriers.

With many diseases, people feel sick before they're most contagious. This makes it easier to identify who should stay home or receive treatment. But with how COVID-19 behaved, it made stopping the spread much harder. Someone could go to work, school, or visit their family without even realizing that they were putting others at risk.

Asymtomatic spread also complicated testing. Early in the pandemic, there weren't many tests available, and they were limited to those who were already sick with symptoms of

COVID-19 MUTATIONS

Viruses change over time, which is known as a mutation. This happens when a virus makes copies of itself. Most mutations don't affect how a virus behaves, but sometimes the mutation can make it more easily spreadable or cause more severe illness.

Because COVID-19 spread quickly, it gave the virus more opportunities to change. Each time the virus infected someone, small genetic changes could occur, which could lead to new virus variants over time.

Variants are versions of a virus that have enough changes to behave differently. Some COVID-19 variants spread faster than earlier versions, while others were better at avoiding the body's immune defenses. This is one of the reasons why COVID-19 case numbers increased again after the numbers had started to go down.

Mutations also made the pandemic harder to predict. Scientists had to constantly study new data to understand each new mutation and if it spread more easily, led to more severe disease, or reacted differently to treatments and vaccines. The new variants also made testing more difficult because there was the chance that the tests may not pick up the new variant. For example, not all the rapid at-home COVID-19 tests picked up the Omicron variant when it first started spreading in 2021.

COVID-19. This meant many infections went **undetected**, allowing the virus to move easily through communities.

Because scientists couldn't rely on symptoms alone, prevention strategies had to change. This is why people were soon asked to wear masks whenever they were around others, gatherings were limited, and physical distancing was implemented to reduce disease spread from anyone, not just those who felt ill.

PROTECTING HIGH-RISK PEOPLE

As scientists learned more about COVID-19, it was clear that it didn't affect everyone the same way. People with preexisting conditions such as asthma, heart disease, diabetes,

There are different types of masks, but the ones that offer the most protection are medical-grade ones. Some people wore masks before the pandemic, and some still wear them now.

FAST FACT

TO ACCOMMODATE THE MASSIVE INCREASE IN COVID-19 PATIENTS IN HOSPITALS, OPERATING ROOMS WERE CHANGED INTO INTENSIVE CARE UNITS (ICUS) AND NON-EMERGENCY SURGERIES WERE POSTPONED TO SAVE BEDS, STAFF, AND EQUIPMENT, AS WELL AS TO PROTECT PATIENTS FROM POSSIBLE EXPOSURE TO THE VIRUS.

cancer, depression, or weakened immune systems were more likely to become seriously ill if infected.

This knowledge shaped many preventative measures, and officials and individuals encouraged people to think of others when it came to ensuring they wore masks and kept a safe distance away from people.

The CDC officially announced that people

should wear a mask when not at home in April 2020. It was in this same month that the CDC announced a new weekly report called "COVIDView," which had information on COVID-19 testing, hospitalizations, and deaths. At this early point in the pandemic, the number of infections had already reached more than 1 million people worldwide.

Measures such as masking and social distancing were also meant to reduce viral load, which is the amount of virus a person is exposed to. Even if someone did become infected,

Because fever is a symptom of COVID-19, it was common for businesses to check temperatures before people were allowed inside, but this did not account for asymptomatic spread.

Seats were closed off on buses with signs such as this one to support social distancing.

exposure to a lower viral load (because the infected person was masking or standing farther away) could mean a milder illness. This was seen as very important for helping people with compromised immune systems.

Signs such as this one encouraged people to wear masks. This practice was common throughout the world during the pandemic.

HOW YOU SEE HISTORY

1. Why do scientists sometimes change their advice?
2. Why was COVID-19 so unpredictable at first?
3. How can uncertainty create a mood of fear or mistrust?

CHAPTER FOUR

ON THE FRONT LINES

When COVID-19 cases started reaching hospitals at a rapid pace, health-care workers found themselves on the front lines of a new and frightening battle. They worked long hours, faced new safety protocols, and tried to help patients who were isolated from their families and dealing with the effects of COVID-19 as well as loneliness from being separated from their loved ones. Working in hospitals during this time was physically exhausting, emotionally draining, and unlike anything that had been experienced before. In another interview with the same anonymous nurse highlighted in Chapter One, she discussed what it was like to work in a hospital during this time and how she tried to help patients who were dealing with loneliness and isolation.

OVERWHELMED HOSPITALS

In early 2020, hospitals became the center of the COVID-19 crisis. Hospitals provided PPE, but even with these items, the fear of becoming infected with COVID-19 was always there. And because health-care workers saw firsthand what COVID-19 did to patients, this fear was worsened. Patient care also changed dramatically. In an interview, the nurse said:

Scan this QR code to watch a nurse talk about what it was like to work in a hospital during the pandemic.

Once we get the patient and they were told they have the COVID, it was kind of very frustrating, very emotional to see them. You can feel how the patient is so scared having the disease. And once they get diagnosed, they were placed in the isolation room by themselves. You see your nurse, depending on how sick [you] are

FAST FACT

IN FEBRUARY 2020, THE CDC STARTED CREATING A COVID-19 TEST. THE FIRST TESTS WERE SENT OUT TO A LAB IN NEW YORK CITY, WITH LAB REPORTS SAYING THE TESTS HAD UNTRUSTWORTHY RESULTS.

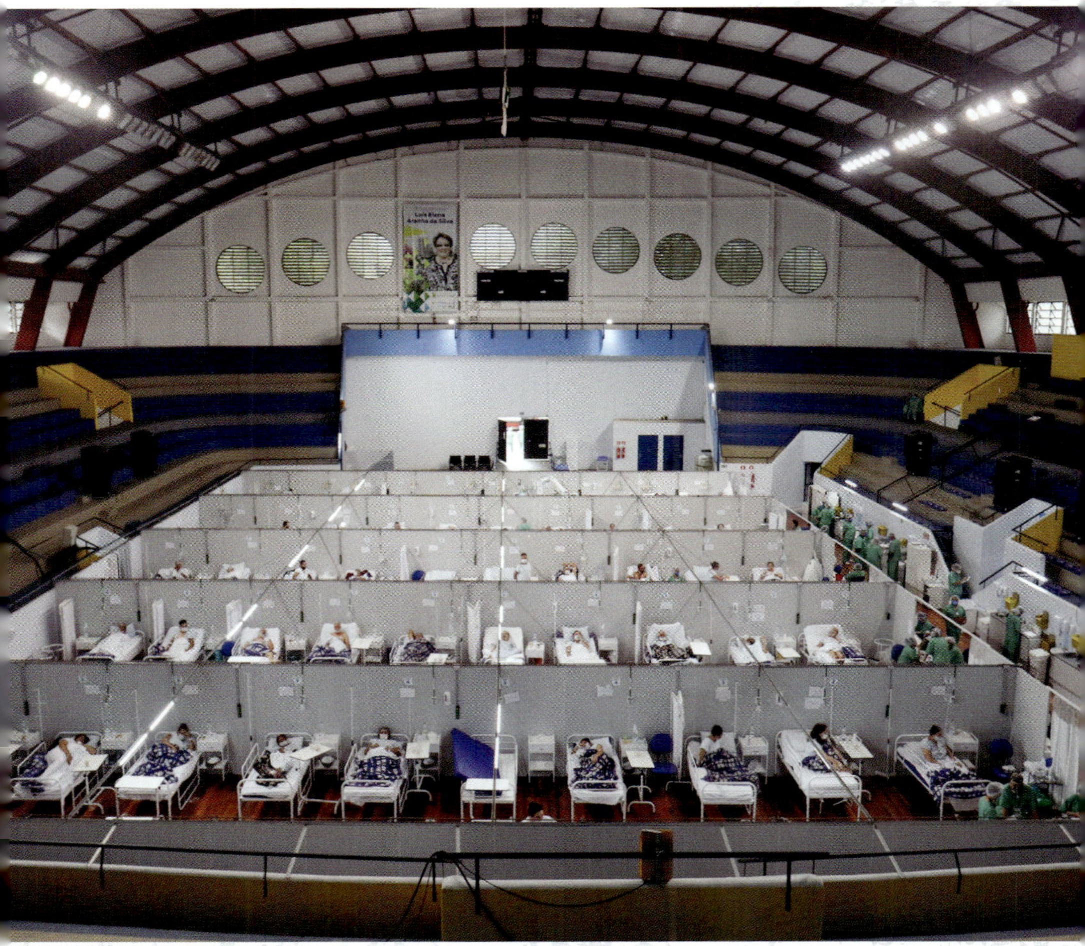

Hospitals were quickly overwhelmed and had to set up makeshift areas to treat COVID-19 patients.

Masks and vaccines were two of the biggest tools used to combat COVID-19, but it took time for a vaccine to be approved.

... And the first few months there was no treatment ... You cannot see your family. The only way we can have them see their family [is] through the iPad that every now and then doesn't work in the room. And during the time we have, sometimes I have to use my own cell phone so I can reach the family if they remember the number. Not all the time that our iPad works for some reason, but our cell phone always works, so we put our cell phone inside the plastic bag and then ... we dial the number for them. And if we're lucky enough, we get ahold of any of the family members. But once they're admitted, nobody can get in the hospital. So that's the saddest thing, especially when they become critical and some decision has to be made.

FAST FACT

CARING FOR VERY SICK PATIENTS EVERY DAY AFFECTED MANY HEALTH-CARE WORKERS' MENTAL HEALTH. MANY EXPERIENCED EXHAUSTION, **BURNOUT**, OR ANXIETY. HOSPITALS LATER INCREASED MENTAL HEALTH SUPPORT SERVICES FOR WORKERS AS THE PANDEMIC CONTINUED.

At first, treatment options were limited. Hospitals tried medications for other illnesses, but nothing was guaranteed to work. They often had to just manage symptoms, such as providing oxygen and administering acetaminophen or ibuprofen for fevers and pain. Because families couldn't visit their loved ones in the hospital, technology was essential. If they could, patients would talk to their families through video calls. Additionally, to prevent spread of the virus to staff members, hospitals would sometimes use video visits or iPads to talk with patients in isolation. This kept health-care workers safer but further isolated patients.

THE RACE FOR A VACCINE

Developing a vaccine generally takes many years because scientists have to first study a virus then design a vaccine that teaches the immune system how to recognize the virus. Before a vaccine (or any treatment) can be released to the public, it also has to go through several steps in clinical trials.

Even though there was a lot of science showing why COVID-19 was real and dangerous, some people still believed COVID-19 wasn't real or a big deal and showed that through graffiti like this.

The first phase is a preclinical study, where the vaccine is tested in a lab and on animals such as mice to see if it triggers an immune response. If the results are promising, the vaccine moves into clinical trials with humans. Phase 1 clinical studies test the safety of the vaccine in a small group of volunteers. Phase 2 studies look for the correct dose and side effects. Phase 3 studies test the effectiveness of the vaccine in a much larger group of people. If all of these studies are promising, the vaccine can start to be manufactured.

Under normal circumstances, these phases happen one after the other, which often takes years. However, during the COVID-19 pandemic, researchers followed

FAST FACT

LOSS OF TASTE AND SMELL IS ONE OF THE SYMPTOMS OF COVID-19 AND WAS OFTEN THE FIRST SYMPTOM THAT MADE PEOPLE NOTICE THEY MAY BE SICK. FOR 90 PERCENT OF PEOPLE, THIS SYMPTOM WENT AWAY IN ABOUT FOUR WEEKS, BUT OTHERS EXPERIENCED LONG-TERM OR PERMANENT CHANGES TO THESE SENSES.

DR. ANTHONY FAUCI

Dr. Anthony Fauci became a well-known, and for many, comforting, figure during the pandemic. As a physician and immunologist, he was the director of the National Institute of Allergy and Infectious Diseases from 1984 until 2022. He also had decades of experience studying diseases such as human immunodeficiency virus (HIV), acquired immunodeficiency syndrome (AIDS), SARS, and Ebola.

During the COVID-19 pandemic, he provided science-backed guidance to the government, health-care workers, and the public. Dr. Fauci also explained how important vaccines were and helped to oversee the development of COVID-19 vaccines. He was an advisor and monitored clinical trials for the Moderna COVID-19 vaccine and others. Dr. Fauci consistently defended the vaccine development process and assured the public that the trials weren't skipping any safety tests. To help build the public's confidence in the vaccine process, he even received his first dose of the Moderna COVID-19 vaccine on television.

To help build further confidence in the vaccines, he explained that the risk and complications of COVID-19 were far greater than the risks of vaccine side effects and that the vaccines had clear safety records based on being tested on thousands of people in the clinical trials.

However, being in the public eye was also very challenging. He faced extreme rhetoric, personal threats, and politically charged backlash, especially when he disagreed with President Donald Trump over the use of hydroxychloroquine (a medication used to treat malaria, lupus, and arthritis) as a treatment for COVID-19. This treatment wasn't effective for COVID-19 and also led to serious side effects that could be fatal.

Dr. Fauci, shown here, was a source of comfort and the voice of reason for many during the pandemic.

Today, Dr. Fauci is mostly out of the public eye. However, for many people, he was a symbol of comfort, truth, knowledge, and scientific leadership in the middle of a frightening time. He was widely regarded as a trusted figure who reassured people through his fact-based explanations of COVID-19.

Vaccine clinics were common once researchers found safe vaccines.

the safety steps, but the processes were expedited because it was a public health emergency. Governments provided funding in advance, enabling companies to manufacture doses while trials were still ongoing. Researchers also built on years of studying coronaviruses and **messenger ribonucleic acid (mRNA)** technology to more quickly produce an effective and safe vaccine.

Some pharmaceutical companies started working on COVID-19 vaccines right away. For example, Moderna began the first human clinical trials of a vaccine in March 2020, developing the vaccine based on years of mRNA research.

By December 2020, COVID-19 vaccines were authorized for emergency use, with health-care workers and people with weakened immune systems or certain preexisting conditions among the first to receive them. Even though the vaccine development timeline was much shorter than usual, the vaccines still met strict safety standards.

To keep track of vaccinations, everyone who got a shot received a vaccine card. The cards included the person's name, vaccine type, date of each dose (the vaccine required more than one dose to reach full effectiveness), and sometimes the vaccine number.

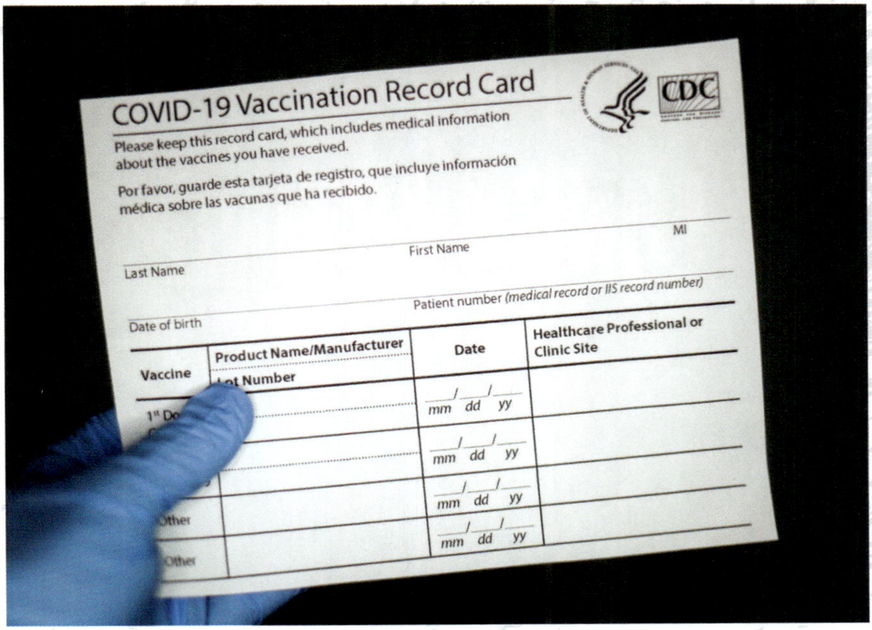

Vaccine cards were used to keep track of doses and to provide proof of vaccination for events.

These cards helped people prove they were vaccinated, which was sometimes necessary, especially as things started to open up and lockdowns ended. For some events or to cross the border from the United States into Canada, for example, proof of vaccination was required.

HOW YOU SEE HISTORY

1. What sacrifices did health-care workers make during the pandemic? Did you know any health-care workers who were working during this time?
2. Why were safe and effective COVID-19 vaccines able to be produced so quickly?
3. Do you think people should have needed to prove they were vaccinated to travel or attend events during the pandemic? Why or why not?

CHAPTER FIVE

LONG-LASTING EFFECTS

The effects of the COVID-19 pandemic weren't just related to overcrowded hospitals and public health rules. Economies slowed down, millions of people lost their lives, and millions more experienced grief from the loss of loved ones and the loss of what life used to be like. Even after an end to the pandemic was declared in May 2023, the effects of this time still impact people today. Many businesses had to close, causing a loss of incomes and careers, and the pandemic had a significant impact on mental health. In another interview with Dr. Koyi Ugboma from 2020, he reflected on how COVID-19 may impact people for years to come.

ECONOMIC IMPACT

The economic effects of COVID-19 were felt immediately. Businesses closed, travel stopped, and people lost their jobs. Some industries, like tourism, entertainment, and restaurants, were hit especially hard. Sporting events and concerts were canceled, and while some were able to be rescheduled, others were completely canceled because rescheduling was impossible. For example, major artists such as Taylor Swift and BTS had concerts and tours canceled because of the pandemic. This led fans to grieve all

Scan this QR code to watch Dr. Koyi Ugboma talk about the effects of the pandemic on society.

Taylor Swift, shown here, wrote her song "Epiphany" to honor health-care workers during the pandemic.

that they missed out on, especially when those things gave them hope. However, the pandemic also led to the creation of new, powerful art inspired by the feelings of isolation experienced at the time.

Governments introduced relief programs to help individuals and businesses survive, but even at the start of the pandemic, people knew the economic impact would be severe. In his 2020 interview, Dr. Ugboma said:

> *I can tell you straight away, it's affecting the economy. I don't know what will happen to the economy in the next five years. I think it's gonna be pretty hard. I think it's going to be from a recession to a depression.*

He worried that the pandemic would lead to a long period of economic hardship, especially because COVID-19 disrupted supply chains and workplaces worldwide. Even years later, the economic impact still remains. Millions of people lost their jobs, and entire industries suffered financial losses that have led to further job losses in the post-pandemic era.

FAST FACT

AS RESTAURANTS STARTED OPENING UP AGAIN, MANY GOT RID OF PAPER MENUS AND STARTED USING QR CODES THAT PEOPLE COULD SCAN TO BRING THE MENU UP ON THEIR PHONE. SOME RESTAURANTS CONTINUED TO USE THIS SYSTEM AFTER THE PANDEMIC ENDED.

The pandemic changed how many people think about travel and increased many people's anxieties around getting sick.

THE TOLL ON HUMAN LIVES

The pandemic also brought widespread grief. It's estimated that 7.1 million people have directly died of COVID-19 as of 2026, but the total of direct and indirect deaths was between 14.9 and 33 million people between 2020 and 2023. This figure includes people who died from COVID-19 and people who died because of factors related to COVID-19, such as health-care system **constraints**. Often, families were unable to gather together to mourn the death of their loved ones or have a traditional funeral during this time.

> **FAST FACT**
>
> DURING THE PANDEMIC, MANY GOVERNMENTS PROVIDED EMERGENCY FINANCIAL HELP, INCLUDING SMALL BUSINESS LOANS, UNEMPLOYMENT BENEFITS, AND CHECKS, TO HELP PREVENT WIDESPREAD POVERTY AND KEEP ECONOMIES FROM COLLAPSING.

Some people who died didn't have family members to claim their body so it could be buried. Their bodies were

Gravediggers often wore PPE while burying those who died from COVID-19 to prevent infection.

taken to a plot of land where they were buried in a mass grave with others who weren't claimed, each person in a plain, unmarked coffin. In his interview, Dr. Ugboma explained:

> *Psychologically, I think people are going to be affected. They lost people. From the African Caribbean society, we attach a lot of importance to the way we bury our dead ... The way they're burying people from this pandemic is they just put people in cremation or they just bury them in mass, which is devastating to a lot of people.*

FAST FACT

SCHOOL CLOSURES IMPACTED STUDENTS' ACADEMICS, BUT MANY STUDENTS ALSO LOST ACCESS TO SCHOOL MEALS (WHICH FOR MANY MAY HAVE BEEN AT NO COST), COUNSELING, AND SOCIAL INTERACTION.

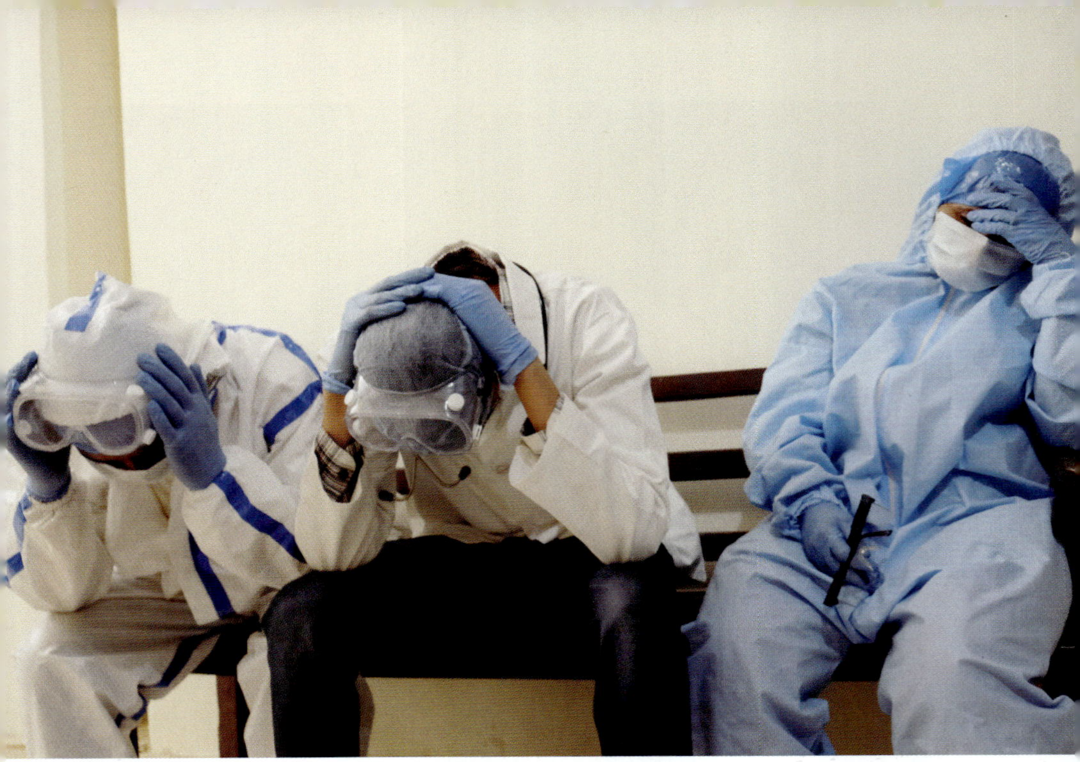

Health-care workers like the one shown here experienced exhaustion after working long shifts.

MENTAL HEALTH IMPACT

The mental health impacts of COVID-19 continue to linger. Many people experienced anxiety, isolation, and fear. Children and teens faced disruption to their schooling during important years, leading some to miss out on important milestones such as high school graduations. Recovery from such widespread trauma takes time.

Back in 2020, Dr. Ugboma was already concerned about how the pandemic would live on in people's memories forever, including his own. He said:

> *I think it's going to live a long time in the memory of so many people. We haven't seen a thing like this in the past. Nobody expected it. And I've been at home for almost three months ... I was one of the first doctors to lose a patient actually from* COVID-19. *So I went to isolation very, very early. I didn't even know what was happening. I was in a state of shock. I was washing my hands every* 10 *minutes. I had hand sanitizers every* 15 *minutes. I had masks. I was even having [a] mask [on] while driving my own car alone.*

LONG COVID

For many people, COVID-19 was an illness that lasted a few days or weeks. However, some people have continued to feel sick long after their initial infection ended. This is known as long COVID.

People with long COVID experience a wide range of symptoms. Some may experience extreme tiredness, trouble concentrating (also called "brain fog"), shortness of breath, headaches, dizziness, and muscle pain. Long COVID can affect adults, children, and teens, including people who weren't seriously ill when they first had COVID-19.

Doctors are still studying why long COVID happens. One theory is that the virus may cause long-lasting inflammation in the body. Another is that COVID-19 impacts the immune or nervous system in a way that takes a long time to heal. There isn't a test to diagnose long COVID, and treatment often focuses on managing symptoms.

Long COVID affects daily life for those who experience it. Some students have struggled to return to school full-time, while adults have had difficulty working or completing everyday tasks that they may have had no trouble with before. The condition has also put additional pressure on the health-care system.

LESSONS FROM THE PANDEMIC

The COVID-19 pandemic revealed the strengths and weaknesses of societies around the world. One important lesson was the value of preparation. Countries with a strong public health system, clear communication, and access to healthcare were often better able to respond quickly to COVID-19.

FAST FACT

MANY HEALTH-CARE WORKERS LEFT THE FIELD BECAUSE OF BURNOUT, ILLNESS, AND EARLY RETIREMENT AFTER THE PANDEMIC. EVEN YEARS LATER, SOME HOSPITALS STILL STRUGGLE WITH LIMITED STAFFING.

The pandemic also showed the importance of scientific research. As scientists learned more about the virus, guidance changed. While this caused confusion at times, it also showed how science improves through the collection of evidence and the adjustment of methods.

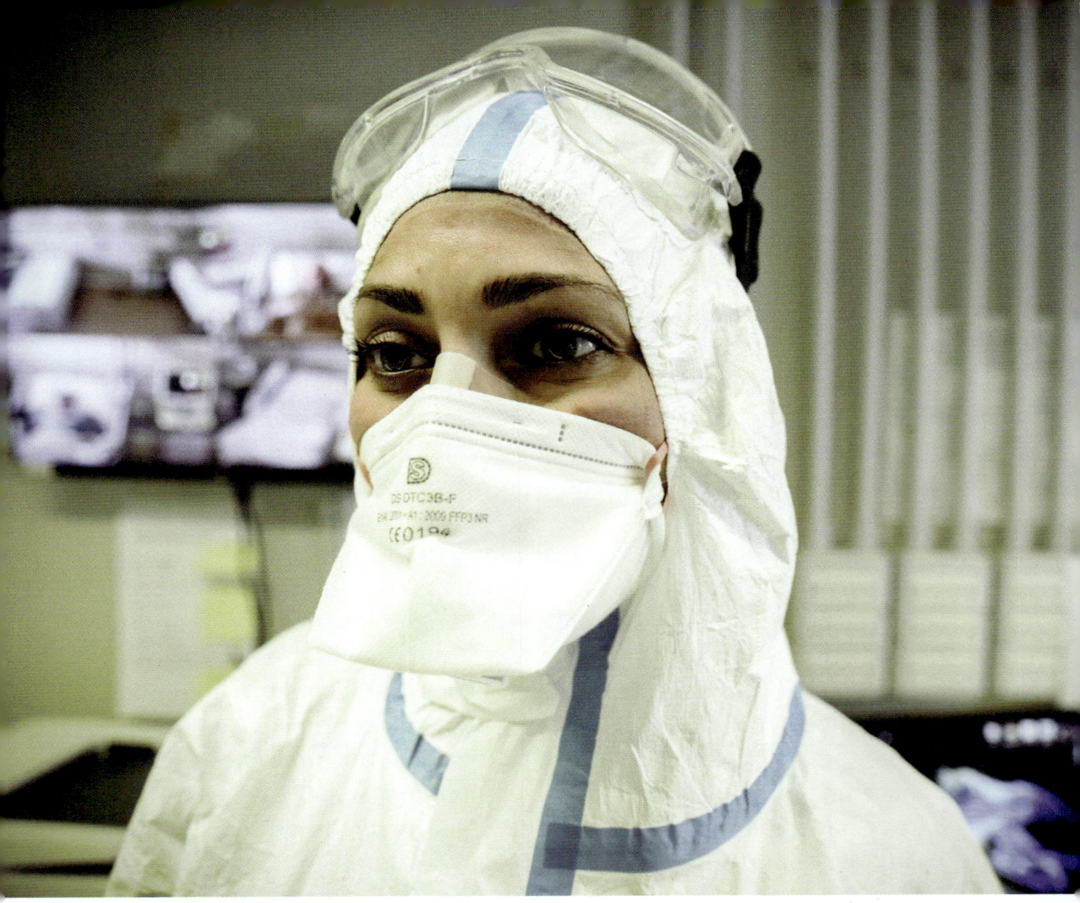

Health-care workers often dealt with bruises on their faces from wearing PPE for long shifts.

As the pandemic came to an end, many people stopped seeing actions such as masking as important. However, wearing a mask is still an effective way to prevent the spread of many sicknesses.

People expressed their appreciation for health-care workers throughout the pandemic with displays such as this one.

COVID also showed the need to address inequality. Some communities were affected more than others, showing how access to health care, safe housing, and stable jobs can shape people's health. Preparing for future crises means strengthening these systems before emergencies happen.

The pandemic also showed how important mental health and social connections are. Isolation, grief, and uncertainty affected nearly everyone in the world. Future preparedness includes not only medical planning, but also ensuring supports are in place for emotional well-being. By learning from the COVID-19 pandemic, societies can better prepare for public health challenges while protecting physical and mental health.

HOW YOU SEE HISTORY

1. How can a pandemic change a society long after it ends?
2. What lessons might future generations learn from the COVID-19 pandemic?
3. How might countries be better prepared for future pandemics?

TIMELINE

A NEW VIRUS: TIMELINE OF THE COVID-19 PANDEMIC

December 2019: A cluster of pneumonia-like diseases appears in Wuhan, China.

January 2020: Scientists confirm a new coronavirus is the reason for the illness in Wuhan.

March 2020: COVID-19 starts spreading across the United States.

THE HUMAN IMPACT: TIMELINE OF THE COVID-19 PANDEMIC

March 2020: States start issuing stay-at-home orders.

HEALTH-CARE AND SCIENCE CHALLENGES: TIMELINE OF THE COVID-19 PANDEMIC

April 2020: The CDC states people should start wearing face masks outside of the home.

April 2020: The number of COVID-19 infections reaches more than 1 million people worldwide.

April 2020: The CDC announces the weekly "COVIDView" report.

ON THE FRONT LINES: TIMELINE OF THE COVID-19 PANDEMIC

February 2020: The first COVID-19 test kits are sent to a lab in New York City but don't produce trustworthy results.

March 2020: Moderna starts human clinical trials for a COVID-19 vaccine.

December 2020: The first vaccines are approved for emergency use.

LONG-LASTING EFFECTS: TIMELINE OF THE COVID-19 PANDEMIC

May 2023: The World Health Organization declares an end to the COVID-19 pandemic.

GLOSSARY

anxiety: A mental health condition marked by strong feelings of fear or nervousness about what might happen.
biological weapon: A disease-causing organism used to harm people on purpose.
burnout: Severe emotional, mental, and physical exhaustion caused by a lot of stress and resulting in extreme tiredness and other mental and physical symptoms.
compromised: When something has been weakened.
consent: To agree to do something.
constraint: A boundary or limitation.
depression: A mental health condition in which a person feels very sad, hopeless, and unimportant and is often unable to do basic tasks because of this.
discrimination: Different—usually unfair—treatment based on factors such as a person's race, age, religion, or gender.
extrovert: Someone who is generally sociable and gains energy by being around others.
genetic engineering: The science of making changes to the basic building blocks of a living thing to produce a desired result.
immunity: Bodily power to resist a disease.
incubation period: The amount of time between when your body is exposed to a germ and when you start feeling sick.
insufficient: Not enough.
marginalized: Relating to people or groups who are treated as unimportant and denied equal access to opportunities or resources.
messenger ribonucleic acid (mRNA): A molecule in the body that carries genetic instructions throughout the body. It acts like a messenger, telling the body to build certain proteins that are needed for cells to function.
mutate: To change.
resigned: The state of accepting a situation because it can't be changed.
resilient: Showing the ability to recover from something.
traumatic: Relating to an event that causes extreme emotional distress.
undetected: Not noticed or found.

FOR MORE INFORMATION

BOOKS

Cross, Paul Ian. *How to Vanquish a Virus*. London, UK: Welbeck Children's Books, 2021.

Goldsmith, Connie. *Understanding Coronaviruses: SARS, MERS, and the COVID-19 Pandemic*. Minneapolis, MN: Twenty-First Century Books, 2022.

Hopkinson, Deborah. *The Deadliest Diseases Then and Now*. New York, NY: Scholastic Books, 2021.

MacKenzie, Debora. *Stopping the Next Pandemic*. New York, NY: Hachette Books, 2020.

Silver, Erin. *What Kids Did: Stories of Kindness and Invention in the Time of COVID-19*. Toronto, ON, Canada: Second Story Press, 2020.

WEBSITES

Coronavirus Disease (COVID-19)
www.who.int/health-topics/coronavirus
Learn more about COVID-19 with articles, fact sheets, and more on the disease and vaccines.

COVID-19
www.britannica.com/science/pandemic
Learn more about the COVID-19 pandemic and vaccines with the help of *Encyclopedia Britannica*.

COVID-19 Pandemic
www.history.com/articles/covid-19-pandemic
Read more about the history of the COVID-19 pandemic at the official website of the History Channel.

History of Infectious Disease Outbreaks and Vaccines
www.mayoclinic.org/diseases-conditions/history-disease-outbreaks-vaccine-timeline
Explore infectious diseases and cures throughout history with the Mayo Clinic.

Stories from the COVID-19 Pandemic: A Resource Guide
guides.loc.gov/covid-19-folklife/library-collections
Explore art, recorded events, and stories from people during the COVID-19 pandemic.

INDEX

PHOTO CREDITS

Cover Drazen Zigic/Shutterstock.com; p. 7 blvdone/ Shutterstock.com; p. 9 H_Ko/shutterstock.com; p. 10 NurPhoto SRL/Alamy Photos; p. 12 Christina Desitriviantie/ Shutterstock.com; p. 13 eldar nurkovic/shutterstock.com; p. 14 Maria Janicki / Stockimo/Alamy Photos; p. 15 Marc Bruxelle/Alamy Photos; p. 16 Prostock-studio/Shutterstock.com; p. 18 Duncan Selby/Alamy Photos; p. 19 Kritthaneth/Shutterstock.coms; p. 20 John David Photography/Shutterstock.com; p. 21 Adam Melnyk/Alamy Photos; p. 22 Matyas Rehak/Shutterstock.com; p. 23 Andrey Maximenko/ Alamy Photos; p. 25 Peter Lopeman/Alamy Photos; p. 26 Andrey_ Popov/Shutterstock.com; p. 27 TT News Agency/Alamy Photos; p. 28 Tupungato/Shutterstock.com; p. 30 Ground Picture/ Shutterstock.com; p. 31 LukeOnTheRoad/Shutterstock.com; p. 32 Thanarak Rerknawa/Alamy Photos; p. 33 Anatoliy Tesouro/ Shutterstock.com; pp. 34, 36 Maridav/Shutterstock.com; p. 37 winnievinzence/Shutterstock.com; p. 38 Mazur Travel/ Shutterstock.com; p. 39 Alena Veasey/Shutterstock.com; p. 41 Brazil Photo Press/Alamy Photos; p. 42 Michael Siluk/ Alamy Photos; p. 44 www.pqpictures.co.uk/Alamy Photos; p. 45 Anthony Fauci 2020/Wikimedia Commons; p. 46 Bignai/ Shutterstock.com; p. 47 Jason Raff/Shutterstock.com; p. 49 ZUMA Press, Inc./Alamy Photos; p. 50 Pradpriew/Shutterstock.com; p. 51 Shutter Photo Press/Shutterstock.com; p. 52 Wirestock, Inc./ Alamy Photos; p. 54 (top) AGENZIA SINTESI/Alamy Photos; p. 54 (bottom) 1Xela/Shutterstock.com; p. 55 Studio 70SN/ Shutterstock.com.

ABOUT THE AUTHOR

NICOLE HORNING is a published author of several nonfiction books for children and teens. She has her Bachelor's degree in English and a Master's degree in education. She doesn't just write for a living; she also enjoys it as a hobby. Nicole loves to collect books and read anything that sounds interesting to her. She also loves learning new things, especially historical topics. She does her best work while listening to Taylor Swift and having one of her two cats in her lap—both things happen a lot.